Cont

Mentoring

A TOOL FOR MINISTRY

HENRY A. SIMON

CPH
SAINT LOUIS

For Dad and Mom

(Philippians 1:3)

1 2 3 4 5 6 7 8 9 10   10 09 08 07 06 05 04 03 02 01

Introduction

"How can we develop leaders in our congregation when everyone is so busy?"

"Is there a way to strengthen the good ministries we have by training team members to assume leadership in the future?"

"We have a problem with new church members walking out the back door six months after they came in the front door to join. What are some options to keep them and help them grow in faith?"

Church leaders ask these kinds of questions as the twenty-first century begins. It's not hard to see why. Personal schedules are tighter, so church sometimes is last on the list of priorities. The "duty" button doesn't work anymore when it comes to "my turn to serve at church." Ease of travel and higher incomes have led more people to go away over weekends, when their parents' pattern would have been to be in town and in worship. Many persons shy away from long-term commitments in any kind of volunteer organization, including church. It's getting harder to find qualified members willing to "build up the body of Christ" by serving in congregations.

But that's not the only problem. Many persons who enter the church as adults don't have any idea of how congregations do ministry. Once upon a time, they could gain that understanding by attending the monthly voters' assembly meeting. But parish structure often has been streamlined, with leadership now in the hands of a smaller elected group serving as a parish council or board of directors. Once upon a time, the values and approaches for effective leadership in a congregation could be understood or "caught" as persons grew up in church, sort of by osmosis. Now many prospective leaders need to be "taught" about serving in and through the church.

All these factors lead to the reason for this book: to offer a tool for ministry to the glory of God and the good of our neighbor. We're going to call that ministry tool "mentoring." This is not a biblical term *per se*, but it can be used to describe a process that takes place in the church between a master and a disciple, guided by the Holy Spirit through the Word of God, which results in an increase of wisdom and better ministry for both.

We need to see this in the context of the offices God has created. Of course it does not replace the divinely ordained Office of the Ministry. Both in the created order and in His Word that created the church, the Lord has established offices into which He places His people. In the created order these offices include fathers and mothers and other authorities. In creating the church, our Lord Jesus Christ endowed it with various offices as well: apostle, pastor, teacher, and so forth. To fill both the created and churchly offices, God calls people into His service and places them into those offices. The Latin word for "call" is *vocare*. Hence, the office or duty to which the Lord calls us is our *voc*ation.

Each vocation is given specific responsibilities from the

Lord Himself. While there is some overlap in duties, there are specific features and attributes of each. Because of the uniqueness of each office, God's people should always know where to turn to receive God's gifts and care.

For example, to receive revelation from God, we look to the apostles and prophets. To receive the means of divine grace—that is, the Word and Sacraments—we turn to pastors. For justice in this sinful world we turn to magistrates and rulers. For the support of home and family we turn to parents and spouses. Each of these people is God's own instrument: the mouth, hands, and voice of God. When they fulfill the duties of their various callings, it is really Christ serving His people.

Within these various offices we can see some common threads and themes that carry through all of the duties. Foremost is that the Word of God defines the nature and duties of the office. Husbands and wives look to Genesis 2:18–24 and find that the Lord has both established and defined their calling to be godly spouses to each other. Likewise, pastors look to John 20. The vocation of the prophet Moses is found in Exodus 3. Acts 9 records the words with which the Lord called the apostle Paul. Every godly vocation is encompassed and endowed by God's Word.

Mentoring is not an office in the church, of course, but the term can be used to describe something that ministers often do in reproducing their ministry in others. Perhaps most significant for our study is that the people of God have often exercised similar methods of living out their vocations and helping others to do so. One of those ways is mentoring.

Here's how we'll approach our goal of describing this tool for ministry:

We'll start with the basics of mentoring as they are understood today.

We'll then explore biblical examples of mentoring.

We'll examine various approaches to mentoring.

We'll meet leaders in Christian congregations who employ mentoring in everything from youth confirmation studies to marriage enrichment to leadership development.

We'll reflect on some true-to-life stories of mentoring.

We'll learn how God's grace can help us through the difficulties of mentoring.

And we'll look at a variety of areas in which mentoring can be used in the congregation.

If you're searching for a way to develop more leaders in your congregation or to strengthen good ministries, this book is intended for you. With the Holy Spirit's blessing, mentoring can be a tool for ministry.

1

Mentoring

Why and How

It was the scariest part of being a new pastor. There I was, facing more than 20 rambunctious junior high students in youth confirmation class. In eight years of college and seminary, including 12 months of "hands on" ministry training in my third seminary year, I had never taught confirmation class. Somehow in all that schooling to become a pastor, teaching junior highs was not required. Now I had no choice. Teaching confirmation was a high-profile part of my pastoral duties.

Thank God that I wasn't in this new experience by myself. My wife of 14 months had agreed to help by team-teaching confirmation class . . . and Mary had the training and experience to go with that offer. In earning her bachelor's and master's degrees in education, she had taught kids from preschool through college.

I still remember how tense I felt before the first confirmation class started on a warm Wednesday afternoon in September 1975. Somehow, I survived. How relaxing it was in the swimming pool afterward! I knew how much I had to learn. But even more, I was grateful that I had a mentor—someone to help me become a teacher. Eventually, I would learn to enjoy interacting with junior high students as we sought to grow in "the grace and knowledge of our Lord and Savior Jesus Christ."

We didn't use the term then, but my wife was mentoring me in how to teach youth confirmation class. Mary reminded me of some basic education theory I had been taught but forgotten. She critiqued my lesson plans and my teaching performance, praising me when I did well and making suggestions when something didn't work. She asked questions that made me think about my goals for that class session and how teenagers would respond. She was a partner who was concerned about my gaining the skills to become a good teacher of junior high students.

After more than 25 years of youth confirmation class, it's now a part of pastoral ministry I really enjoy. In time, I, who began as a humble trainee, became a teacher myself. For a number of years I mentored seminarians, giving them experience as confirmation class aides. After that, these future pastors would not have sweaty palms in their first weeks of confirmation teaching. The "mentee" had become the mentor. Thanks, Mary! And thanks be to God.

Mentors Enrich Life

While your story is different, you can probably think of mentors who have enriched your life. Mary wasn't the first mentor in my life, nor the last. I remember the copy editors on my hometown daily newspaper. They trained me to write a sentence that conveyed action in a sparse but strong style for a news story. They said the mentoring that I received while I worked in the newsroom during college and seminary summers was worth a bachelor's degree in journalism. Thanks, Reiny, Dick, and Don!

Then there was the leader in our congregation who mentored me in personnel matters as we added staff. Administration was not a course required in college or seminary for future pastors—especially not the management of staff. But having a mentor to meet with, reflect with, and learn from was a real blessing. And he continues to help me improve. Thanks, Don!

This book is intended to help you, as a leader in a Christian congregation, use mentoring as a tool for ministry. In these pages you will learn about various ways of helping others that come under the umbrella term "mentoring." You will meet leaders of churches that use mentoring to help their members grow in their Christian faith and life. You will have the opportunity to reflect on how you have been mentored . . . and think about whom you might mentor.

Mentoring can be used in a variety of ways to help Christians be more effective in sharing the Good News of Jesus Christ through their words and actions. You're invited to share in a journey as we learn more about mentoring as a tool for ministry.

The Original Mentor

Mentors take their name from a mythical character in Homer's ancient Greek epic poetry. Mentor was a soldier and friend of the hero Odysseus. But "he" really was a "she"—the goddess Athena in disguise. She assumed Mentor's form to help Odysseus, his wife Penelope, and their son Telemachus in a variety of tests and trials. While we as Christians reject pagan religion, we can study ancient myths with profit insofar as they contain truth. The truth contained in the story of Mentor is that divine guidance can come through an older and wiser friend.

The name *mentor* has henceforth been used to describe someone who assists or helps another person who is less experienced or skilled. Some experts suggest the synonym of coach or guide. Mentoring could be described as a kind of teaching, something like apprentices once experienced as they stood next to their masters and learned a trade.

We don't hear much about apprentices anymore. When mentoring is done in the way that experts describe, the boss-employee relationship takes on an aspect of genuine concern more for the person than even for the performance of a job. Maybe that's why the term *mentor* can describe someone who helps another person reach his or her God-given potential in using skills and abilities.

It hasn't always been that way. Our conception of mentoring has changed quite a bit in recent years. Back in 1988, our family paid a hefty sum to purchase a complete set of the *Encyclopedia Britannica* for use by our three children in homework. However, by the time the youngest reached high school in 1995, the Internet was becoming the preferred source of information. This change also holds true in learning about mentoring. That encyclopedia I bought does not have an entry under "mentoring." But the local library or bookstore carries a number of books on the subject. If you search the Internet you will be referred to hundreds of sites dealing with mentoring. They range from helping children at risk to mentoring Native American students in scientific fields to assisting persons interested in commercial flight training. Mentoring is with us to stay.

Why Mentoring?

While Mentor himself was Greek, we find that the Bible contains examples of what can be called mentoring. Instances of older, more experienced men equipping people to face future challenges are included in the next seven chapters.

Somehow in modern society we have lost the naturalness we find in the Bible of a more experienced person helping another gain skills or understanding. In a society where the average family moves twice in a decade and McDonald's and Taco Bell may provide as many meals as the family stove, the time or availability for once-assumed relationships has vanished. Many children no longer learn how to fish from grandpa; few are helped with homework by their parents at the kitchen table. A young person can go through grade school and high school without a significant one-on-one relationship with a teacher. An increasing amount of learning happens through computers and the Internet, which open a treasure trove of information but eliminate the relational aspect of learning from a human teacher face-to-face.

Mentoring provides an opportunity for Christians to go back to a relationship where one person (the mentor) cares enough about another person (the mentee) to invest valued time, precious energy, and emotional and mental effort in him or her. Dr. J. Robert Clinton has spent much of his professional time in recent years in performing, analyzing, and writing about mentoring. As a seminary professor, he views mentoring as a tool to be used by Christians in helping one another. He says that mentoring is one person helping another person to grow. This happens as the mentor transfers resources to the mentee, including knowledge, skills, and networking. These make resources available for developing God-given potential, considering new habits, and establishing values for living.[1]

Dr. Clinton spreads the umbrella of mentoring wider than other writers on the subject. He sees mentoring involved when one person disciples another, serves as a spiritual director, or coaches another person in developing abilities. He also considers counseling a form of mentoring, as well as teaching or being a sponsor to someone in his or her career. He proposes three final types of mentoring, which do not even involve contact with another person. One is using a contemporary leader as a model (including one whom you've never met). Another is learning about the life of a historical figure, usually from a biography. The last is seeing God intersect your life with divine guidance that moves you to fulfill His will for you.[2]

But Is It Mentoring?

Other authorities disagree with Dr. Clinton. Some feel that helping a person grow in faith through one-on-one conversations, Bible study, and spiritual disciplines does not qualify as mentoring. The Center for Coaching & Mentoring, Inc., distinguishes coaching from mentoring. This is based on a 1998 online survey that asked whether persons who had been mentored felt there was a difference between a mentor, coach, and supervisor. According to Dr. Matt M. Starcevich, persons involved in mentoring saw it as an arrangement in which participants are equals and seek to learn together. The mentor helps the mentee in a low-key way, drawing on understanding and skills gained by experience.[3] Coaching, on the other hand, was perceived as part of supervisory techniques used to help do a job more effectively and efficiently. Coaching was seen as job-related and performance driven, sometimes imposed on a person, while mentoring was a choice made by someone to have an affirming relationship that focused on the person.[4]

In the final analysis, defining what is involved in mentoring is helpful so that a mentor and mentee share an understanding of what is expected by both of them. Who cares whether something is technically considered mentoring or not? The bottom line is that the relationship providing growth (in faith, understanding, or abilities) is offered and the person on the receiving end benefits.

The "How" of Mentoring

In *Mentoring: A Practical Guide* Gordon F. Shea indicates that mentoring involves going farther in a relationship than would normally be expected. He believes that a mentor will draw upon experience, skills, and understanding to teach, counsel, guide, and help another person in individual and professional development.[5] This concept gives us a starting point to think about the "how" of mentoring.

Being a mentor means having something to share with another who needs it to help him grow. In most cases, experts agree, this mentoring happens informally. But if it is mentoring, Shea says, a primary factor usually is that the mentee approaches the mentor. Even when the situation is reversed, the mentee is free to choose whether to be mentored or not.

The United States Coast Guard says that mentoring begins when the two partners put expectations of the relationship in writing. They build on this agreement by developing a realistic plan to help the mentee reach specific goals. As the mentee begins to grow, the mentor backs off so that the mentee can discover answers on his or her own. The mentor asks questions, encourages the mentee to take risks, alerts him to possible new strategies, and serves as guide and counselor.[6] The Coast Guard goes on to say that five elements are essential in what it terms "successful mentoring connections": respect, trust, realistic expectations, partnership building, and time.[7]

Dr. Clinton mentors intentionally and has developed administrative helps. He may require mentees to write him after a meeting, listing what the mentee and Clinton will be doing before the next meeting. Mentees often are asked to write an agenda for these meetings. When Dr. Clinton wants to establish a relationship with a mentee that will be long term, he writes a letter that spells out what goals he sees as possible for the potential mentee and what he can do to help. This forms the basis for negotiating the mentoring relationship.[8]

In the Congregation

As a leader who wishes to mentor (and to be mentored), you and the other person will need to decide how structured you wish to make your relationship. Few of us will be as structured as Dr. Clinton.

That's because much of our mentoring will be informal and occasional. But if you are intentionally mentoring another person, as I have mentored an assistant pastor just graduated from the seminary, putting expectations in writing is crucial. If you fail to agree on the goal and strategy for the relationship, you can end up spending much time, energy, and effort with little return on your investment. That's not good stewardship. But if you are willing to invest yourself in mentoring, you will be doing your best to help another Christian develop God-given abilities and use the resources that the Lord of the church provides for His people. That can make mentoring worthwhile.

2

Mentoring to Share Experience

Jethro and Moses

Moses wouldn't seem like someone who would need to enroll in Leadership 101 at the Mt. Sinai Seminary. Look at his resume:
— Used by God to convince one of the mightiest kings of the day to release a nation of slaves who had served for hundreds of years.
— Led the Israelites on their journey to freedom.
— Received the Ten Commandments on stone tablets from God on the holy mountain.

Yet when Moses' father-in-law, Jethro, visited the Israelites several months into the exodus, it was clear that Moses could use some help. Moses' problem was a familiar dilemma for persons who move into administration and can't seem to find enough time to do all the work. "When his father-in-law saw all that Moses was doing for the people, he said, 'What is this you are doing for the people? Why do you alone sit as judge, while all these people stand around you from morning till evening?'" (Exodus 18:14).

Like many of us who get in over our heads with the

work of the Lord, Moses had a ready answer: "Because the people come to me to seek God's will" (v. 15). If we are overloaded with too much church work, odds are that we have forgotten just whose work it is: the Lord's, not ours. We may defend what we're doing because we think God has told us to do it that way. Usually that's not the case. That's the point behind Jethro's suggestion to Moses. The old priest of Midian doesn't mince words with the younger leader: "What you are doing is not good. You and these people who come to you will only wear yourselves out. The work is too heavy for you; you cannot handle it alone" (v. 17–18).

There it is, out in the open, plainly stated. No one is indispensable in the work of the Lord, not even someone as impressive as Moses. So Jethro suggested that Moses continue to be the people's representative before God, but personally handle only the difficult cases. For simple disputes, Jethro suggested that Moses appoint officials over groups of thousands, hundreds, fifties, and tens, apparently functioning as a court system with a number of appeal levels. That's what happened. As a result, we read that "capable men" also were able to use their talents as leaders and Moses' representatives.

Moses would face many tests and trials for almost 40 more years of his people's wilderness wandering. But no longer would he have to serve as judge for every dispute. The mentoring of his father-in-law, Jethro, had assured that.

For reflection:

1. Have you ever found yourself overloaded with church

work, yet didn't know how you could disengage yourself from your predicament? What happened?

2. Why are pastors or other church leaders especially vulnerable to make mistakes if they, like Moses, say, "the people come to me to seek God's will"?

3. Why was Jethro able to be a good mentor for Moses?

4. Jethro made only one suggestion to Moses, yet it impacted his life for the rest of the exodus journey. What does this say about the best time frame for helpful mentoring?

Exploring the Concept

Mention the word "mentor" and many people will think about the kind of relationship that Jethro had with Moses. Mentoring traditionally has been associated with an experienced person taking a new person under her wing for training. The concept of apprentice still is used in some construction trades to designate a person who is learning the skills from a veteran. Even when the help is short-term, such as Jethro's, it still is mentoring.

Mentoring to share the knowledge and skills gained by experience can be short-term or long-term, depending on the goal. Age does not limit how such mentoring takes place. One example is the mentoring of junior high confirmation students by adults and senior high school students at St. John Lutheran Church, Ellisville, Missouri. Although Rev. Peter Mueller admits that the mentoring idea "was born out of necessity" to keep order among the 120 seventh and eighth graders in the program, he is convinced that this approach has worked well.

The associate pastor divides the junior high students into small groups, with an average of one adult for every five to nine students. The mentors lead the groups in their studies. This includes working with each student before he or she makes a presentation on one of the Six Chief Parts of Martin Luther's Small Catechism in a special service involving the confirmands. The mentor works with the student for five weeks, asking probing questions about the catechism teaching involved to help the student formulate the presentation.

High school students were added as apprentice mentors when Mueller saw that new confirmands were ready to make an investment in terms of their faith. "It's hard for teens to find ways to pass on their faith," he notes, "except to younger kids." Now that's happening, as senior high students work with the adults to mentor the junior high kids in the small groups.

Mentoring is an important concept at Our Savior Lutheran Church, Arcadia, California, where Rev. Roger Sonnenberg uses it to strengthen the ministry to couples in the engagement and "just married" stages of life. He came up with the idea while reading the apostle Paul's instructions that the older women "can train the younger women to love their husbands and children" (Titus 2:4).

The concept begins with couples who have been married for a number of years volunteering to serve as mentors. Sonnenberg holds a 90-minute training session with them, usually in the fall. Then he matches mentoring couples with engaged couples who are beginning marriage preparation sessions with him. Both couples sign a contract spelling out what is expected of the mentors and the couple approaching marriage. Mentors first meet with the couple seven to eight months before the wedding date. They provide advice as the wedding approaches. Some become so much a part of the bridal couple's extended family that they have been asked to participate in the wedding service in ways such as reading the Scripture lessons.

The mentoring is "absolutely wonderful," one couple recently told Sonnenberg. Mentors and the mentee couples meet twice a year for discussions, but the mentors are available also at other times. Some mentors enjoy the arrangement so much that they mentor more than one set of newlyweds. Their enjoyment also was reflected in the fact that in the first six years of the approach, none of the mentors asked to end their volunteering in this way. The mentoring approach has been so successful that Sonnenberg has been asked by other congregations to lead workshops on the program.

A Slice of Life

Larry watched how Juan was interacting with the preschoolers running across the church lawn, looking for brightly colored eggs nestled in the grass. The youth group was working with the Sunday school on the Saturday before Easter to sponsor an egg hunt as a community outreach event.

Many of the teens were standing on the sidewalk at the edges of the activity, trying to make sure they didn't get their shoes wet from the dewy grass. But Juan was wandering around with the younger children, pointing out eggs to those whose baskets were empty, encouraging others who weren't keen on being part of the hunt, and generally being a help. As the congregation's director of Christian education, Larry knew that being able to relate to young children was a gift that not everyone possessed.

So he wasn't surprised at what he learned when he met with Juan, who was part of that spring's confirmation class. Larry had led the group in a study of spiritual gifts mentioned in the Bible. Then the confirmands had thought back over their lives and noted the abilities with which God seemed to have blessed them. Larry's role was to discuss those abilities with the students, suggesting ways in which they could serve as part of becoming adult members in the congregation. He noticed that Juan's sheet indicated that he felt gifted in teaching and in caring for others.

"I see that you're interesting in teaching, Juan," Larry said during their conversation. "Would you be interested in trying your hand at Sunday school teaching, to see if this may be an area in which you can serve the Lord in church?"

"You know, I've thought about helping out in Sunday school," Juan replied. "Do you think I could do it?"

Larry paused a bit, then responded, "Well, you wouldn't be in it alone. I'll ask Mrs. O'Connor if you could work with her. She teaches our four-year-old class. That would be an excellent way to find out whether teaching is a 'fit' for you, as well as learning from a master teacher. It's what some people might call mentoring."

Juan agreed to give it a try, so Larry made arrangements with Mrs. O'Connor. Over the following months, Juan learned much about what makes a good teacher. He already possessed an attitude of enjoying people and a willingness to listen to others. Mrs. O'Connor showed him how to write a lesson plan, adapting suggestions from the curriculum's teacher's guide to their situation. She rescued him from several situations where preschoolers were acting up, as she modeled how to handle them gently but firmly. She helped him to absorb the kind of caring and flexibility that was necessary with a lively group of children who just couldn't wait to "go to school" all day by beginning kindergarten the following year.

The day came when Mrs. O'Connor said to Juan, "I think it's time that we move into team teaching, if you'd be willing. You have learned enough that we can teach together, with you leading one week and my assisting, then switching the next week. This also will give us the opportunity to take a Sunday off now and then to sit in on a Bible class."

"I'd be happy to do that, Mrs. O'Connor," Juan replied. "But I'd still like to be able to ask you for help and ideas when I get stuck. I don't want to give you up as my mentor entirely."

"That would be fine, Juan," she responded. "I can continue to mentor when you need that, but our relationship has changed since you started on the Sunday school staff. It's been a joy for me to mentor you, as you grew in teaching skills."

For reflection:

1. Has someone more experienced ever helped you learn new skills and understanding? What were the circumstances?

2. Is there some area in church where you would be interested in serving, for which you would like mentoring? Is there someone you could ask to mentor you?

For action:

One reason that some persons do not volunteer to serve at church is that they are afraid they do not have the skills or experience needed. A veteran worker offering to "give them a taste" of that ministry by serving with them sometimes can convince them to try it. If the person decides to continue in the ministry, a mentoring relationship then can develop.

Think about one area in your congregation where you would be willing to mentor someone who is interested in serving there, but lacks experience. Talk to the person leading the ministry about your idea.

3

Mentoring to Prepare for Leadership

Moses and Joshua

Joshua watched the 120-year-old Moses stride across the plain toward Mt. Nebo. Now Joshua would succeed Moses as leader of the Israelites. He recalled the way in which Moses would talk to him about decisions to be made and the challenges of leadership. And Joshua reflected that 40 years had been a long time to wait for the word of the Lord that Moses finally had spoken, promising God's presence with Joshua as he assumed leadership.

Joshua remembered the first battle the Israelites had fought on the exodus. Moses had appointed him to command the Lord's people after the Amalekites had attacked them. The Israelites had won, with God's help. Then Moses had honored Joshua by appointing him as his aide (Exodus 24:13). He would spend 40 years learning from Moses.

Joshua frowned as he remembered the trip of the 12 spies to explore Canaan, the land promised by God to His people. When the spies had discovered powerful heathen tribes living there, only he and Caleb had urged the people to trust in God to help them conquer the land. But the people had been too afraid. The other 10 spies were now dead, because God's punishment was to declare that no one 20 years or older would enter the Promised Land, except for Joshua and Caleb (Numbers 13, 14). Another honor had come to Joshua when Moses constructed the Tent of Meeting as a place for him to consult with the Lord God before the tabernacle was built. Joshua recalled the many nights he had stayed in the tent, guarding it against intruders (Exodus 33:11). He knew that he had experienced the defeats and the delights of leadership, watching Moses lead his nation as no other man would ever do.

It was in Moses' three addresses to the Israelites before he died, Joshua reflected, that his mentoring finally had come to an end. Moses began by telling the people that he would not be allowed to enter the Promised Land, because of his sin at Meribah. It had been 40 years since the people's rebellion against entering Canaan. God had told Moses that Joshua would succeed Moses as leader, guiding the Israelites into their inheritance (Deut. 1:38). Moses ended his initial recitation of the Israelites' history by repeating the words of the Lord about his aide: "Commission Joshua, and encourage and strengthen him, for he will lead this people" (Deut. 3:28).

That commissioning had just taken place (Deut. 31:14), including Moses' laying of hands on Joshua. Now Moses, his mentor, was walking to his death. Joshua knew that his turn to lead the people had come.

Does 40 years seem like a very long time to be "leader in waiting"? We might think so, but we don't know if Joshua chafed at growing into an old man before he could assume leadership. His task as a leader of God's people would be second in difficulty only to what Moses, his mentor, faced. Moses was called by God to lead the people out of slavery in Egypt, through the Red Sea and the wilderness, to the Promised Land. It would be Joshua's job to conquer the heathen inhabitants of his people's inheritance, divide the land between the 12 tribes, and oversee the settling of a nomadic people into a country of farmers and herders.

You could call Joshua the best-prepared leader ever to serve as judge for the Israelites. Moses was up to the task of mentoring Joshua to prepare for that leadership. We see this mentoring again and again in the first five books of the Bible. The fourth to last verse in Deuteronomy records: "Now Joshua, son of Nun, was filled with the spirit of wisdom because Moses had laid his hands on him. So the Israelites listened to him and did what the Lord had commanded Moses" (Deut. 34:9).

Joshua went on to lead the Israelites into Canaan. He won victories with God's help and lived up to the meaning of his name, "The Lord saves." Centuries later, this name would be given to the son of Mary who also was the Son of God, the Christ. In modern Hebrew, it is Yeshua; in English, Jesus. He would be a leader greater than the first Joshua, and greater even than Moses. As the angel said, Jesus would "save His people from their sins."

For reflection:

1. Do you think that Joshua ever grew tired of being mentored by Moses during those 40 years of wandering in the wilderness? Have you ever been trained for assuming leadership and grown tired of waiting to take over?

2. How did Joshua's experiences help prepare him for leadership?

3. Why was it important that Moses tell the people about God ordering the commissioning of Joshua? Besides commissioning Joshua, what else was Moses to do for his successor?

4. What ideas about mentoring can you learn from Joshua's experience with Moses?

Exploring the Concept

Despite what some people may think, leaders are made, not born. That includes persons whom congregations elect to lead them. Often the person elected as congregational president will have served in other positions, providing an opportunity for a nominating committee to assess personal style and leadership abilities.

Gethsemane Lutheran Church, Tempe, Arizona, provides another alternative. Its members elect someone to be trained as president. The office of president-elect involves the duties that most congregations assign to a vice president. But the person is chosen for a two-year term. During the first year, the current president is expected to mentor the president-elect. That prepares the president-elect to head the congregation as president in the second year.

There are obvious advantages to this arrangement, according to Rev. John Krueger, senior pastor at Gethsemane. But the president needs to be committed to the time involved in the mentoring process. If problems arise in a congregation, the president will need to spend time not only dealing with them but also continuing the mentoring of the president-elect.

Professional church workers also are seeing the need for mentoring lay leaders. This has led to a program called Developing Leaders for Ministry (DLM), which was begun in The Lutheran Church—Missouri Synod in the early 1990s. DLM uses the model of servant leadership developed by Robert Greenfield, according to Rev. Dr. J. Arthur Cox, DLM national director and pastor of Grace Lutheran Church, Bradford, Pennsylvania.

DLM began with pastors, directors of Christian education, and other church professionals meeting in clusters about 12 times a year. Led by a facilitator, participants spend 90 minutes on leadership development and another half an hour in prayer. They talk about their experiences as persons and professional church workers, while also providing support for one another. Once a year, all DLM facilitators meet for a 48-hour national conference to be mentored themselves. Together, they were serving as group mentors for almost 300 church professionals at the start of the century.

Cox was excited that the year 2000 marked the next stage in the leadership development plan. At this time, the professionals would be encouraged to "move a level up to the lay leadership" by in turn mentoring them. He indicated that this has been tried in several places on a trial basis and has worked well.

The ultimate goal of DLM is to do better at achieving the goal of "reaching the lost," according to Cox, by mentoring people to use leadership as a tool for outreach.

Rev. Dennis Conrad agrees with Cox. An enthusiastic cluster leader for DLM in upstate New York, Conrad conducts monthly training sessions for his lay leaders at St. John Lutheran Church, Orchard Park, New York. "Leadership is the most important thing that pastors do" to build on Word and Sacrament ministry and be in mission for Jesus Christ, Conrad says. He adds that in the twenty-first century, ministry will need to be done by leaders in the congregation, not just by pastors.

As an example, Conrad points to his goal of never doing ministry alone, but always having someone accompany him, so he can mentor that person. Each Monday, Conrad takes a layperson with him on hospital calls, teaching his companion how to do such visits. The New York pastor notes that part of using the DLM pattern is to teach a congregation that ministry (in the broad sense of Christian serving) doesn't just come from the pastor. The Holy Spirit has given a variety of gifts to God's people, the New Testament teaches, so that they can build up the body of Christ, the church.

"It's a risk to share leadership with members," Conrad says. "And it's hard to get this kind of thing started. But you really are only half a leader until you give some of that leadership away." Like Moses with Jericho, modern day leaders of God's people know the wisdom of mentoring to prepare others for leadership.

A Slice of Life

Steve shifted uncomfortably in his chair as the rest of the elders glanced at him. He had been afraid that something like this might happen ever since he had noticed the item "preparing for next chairperson" on the agenda mailed to him earlier in the week. He knew that Sam, the current chair, could serve on the board only one more year, owing to term limits specified in the bylaws. Steve also knew that he was next in seniority on the board and the logical person to chair the elders during the following year.

"As we're all aware," Sam said, "I have only one year left to serve on the elders. While I'm willing to continue as chairperson, I think it would be good to have someone I could work with follow me as chair. Steve, you've served on the board longer than anyone besides me. Would you be willing to prepare to serve as chairman next year if I mentor you this year? We could elect you as vice chair, with the understanding that you would become chairman next year. What do you think?"

Steve shifted some more, before he looked up and saw the approving smiles of his fellow elders. "They really do want me to prepare to lead this board," he thought to himself. Then he put his thoughts into words. "Yes, I'd be willing to be elected vice chairperson, with two understandings," Steve said. "First, Sam will help bring me up to speed on what it means to chair the board and serve as its leader. And second, if during my being vice chair I see that I'm not cut out to be chairperson, I can tell you and someone else can fill my shoes. If that's agreeable, I'll serve." The other elders agreed, and Sam began mentoring Steve.

It started by Sam meeting with Steve to go over the duties of the elders and the way they served in the congregation, assisting with Communion and Baptisms and overseeing membership actions. Steve was aware of all of this and of Sam's insistence that the best way in which the elders served was by being responsible for the support and well-being of their pastor. Sam also mentored Steve in preparing the agenda for the monthly elders' meeting, with input from the pastor. Steve went along with Sam to a council meeting, learning how Sam presented the recommendations of the elders and served as spokesperson for one of the senior boards in the congregation.

Early in the fall, before the nominations committee had started work, Steve and Sam met with the pastor to discuss future service by the elders and to answer any questions that Steve still had. When Steve finally was installed with the other board members and officers on the first weekend in January, he felt that Sam had mentored him well. He was ready to assume leadership as chairperson of the board of elders.

For reflection:

1. Have you ever been in a position where it seemed that you were next in line to be the leader? How did you feel about it?

2. How can mentoring provide training in skills, understandings, and attitude for a potential new leader in a congregational ministry?

3. Was it important that Steve had an "escape clause" in his verbal contract to serve as vice chairperson, preparing to be the next chairperson? Why?

For action:

Some organizations have an understanding that a vice chairperson or assistant coordinator moves up to the next position automatically. Yet sometimes this is not spelled out in writing. Others have created a position of "president-elect" or something similar to make it clear that the next leader currently is being mentored. If you feel this is a good idea to consider, talk to the president of your congregation, the chairperson of your board, or the leader of your ministry team to see if this could be discussed.

4

Mentoring to Grow in Faith

Priscilla and Aquila and Apollos

Imagine using a computer keyboard or typewriter that has only the top row of letters. It's true that you have keys for some of the most important letters, like *t* and *e* and *o*. You can put together some important words, like *write* and *power* and *reap*. But because you are missing two other lines of letters, not to mention the row of numbers and signs at the top of the keyboard, you are limited in any story you seek to tell, no matter how skillful you are in typing.

That's one way of thinking what it was like for Apollos as he traveled through Asia Minor (modern Turkey) preaching about the coming Jewish Messiah, the Savior of the world. Apollos had been born in Alexandria, an Egyptian city where the Old Testament of his people had been translated from Hebrew into Greek, the commercial language of the day. He was an excellent student of the Scriptures and a good speaker. He was a disciple of John the Baptizer, the prophet who had been martyred for standing up to the wicked king Herod. John preached a baptism of repentance as a way to prepare for the coming Savior, and so did Apollos.

In his journey through Turkey he came to the important city of Ephesus. In the Jewish synagogue there, Apollos began to speak and teach with great vigor. His words were eloquent, but all he knew about the Christ was what John the Baptizer said about Him. We can't even be sure that Apollos knew that John had pointed to Jesus as the Lamb of God who would take away the sins of the world.

That was like typing with only the top row of a keyboard. For not only had Jesus come, He had lived a perfect life, died on the cross, risen from death, and returned to His Father in heaven, sending the Holy Spirit to guide His disciples. Imagine the joy in Apollos' heart when Priscilla and Aquila invited him to their home and began to explain to him the rest of the story!

They mentored him as they "explained to him the way of God more adequately," Luke reports (Acts 18:26). Now Apollos, to use our image, had use of the entire keyboard. Now he could tell the complete story of God's great love, expressed in sending His Son Jesus to be the Savior of the world. He could proclaim not only the promised Messiah but also the Suffering Servant of the Lord predicted by Isaiah and the living Redeemer about whom Job spoke. Apollos could share the whole story, showing those prophecies and being more fulfilled in Jesus.

That's what Apollos began to do. He wanted to go to the Greek province of Achaia, where Athens was located. So the Christians wrote letters of introduction to the believers there and encouraged Apollos to continue his missionary efforts. Upon arriving there, Luke reports, "he was a great help to those who by grace had believed"(Acts

18:27). A key part of his work was to use the Old Testament to show that Jesus was indeed the promised Savior.

Apollos also visited Corinth at least twice and Ephesus once more. Martin Luther and others have even suggested that Apollos went on to write the anonymous Letter to the Hebrews. Whether that is the case or not, we can be sure that throughout the rest of his life Apollos continued to share the faith in which he had been mentored by Priscilla and Aquila.

For reflection:

1. Someone has suggested that parents are our first mentors in learning to believe in Jesus as the Savior. Was this true in your case? Who else has been a mentor to you in growing in the faith?

2. From Luke's account, it does not sound like Priscilla and Aquila said to Apollos, "Stop right now! You're wrong in what you're preaching about John the Baptizer and the baptism for repentance. Let us tell you the correct story." Instead, they invited Apollos into their home and explained to him about Jesus. What does their method of mentoring say about how we help others grow in the faith?

3. Priscilla and Aquila were tentmakers, like the apostle Paul. Apollos probably was more educated and a better public speaker than they. What does his willingness to be mentored by them say about what's important in finding someone to mentor yourself to grow in the faith?

A Slice of Life

If there ever was a time in the life of the Christian church in America for mentoring to help spread the faith, it is now. The twenty-first century presents an opportunity for one-on-one and small-group mentoring to share the living water that Jesus Christ offers to a spiritually thirsty culture.

When someone is led by the Holy Spirit to come or return to active faith, notes veteran mentor David Kraft, "usually someone has come alongside them and encouraged them" to consider the claims of Jesus Christ. That's not as natural as it was half a century ago, because our culture has an anti-Christian bias, as well as a distorted image of what the Bible teaches. Kraft feels that Hollywood, television, and the media are responsible. Another obstacle is that many young adults have little or no knowledge of the message and claims of the Bible. Remember the Jay Leno survey in which some people indicated that Joan of Arc was the wife of Noah?

New Christians often ask, "Where do I go from here?" Kraft says. He developed a program to meet this need of new believers while working in discipleship ministry at Our Savior Community Lutheran Church, Palm Springs, California. He began by training a group of potential members much like "counselors" are prepared at Billy Graham Crusades to meet with seekers. Then, Kraft would pair a new believer and a trained veteran member with the goal of mentoring the new Christian. This mentoring relationship provided the opportunity for the new members to ask questions and learn about the basics of the faith. It also introduced them to spiritual disciplines such as prayer and devotional time to help them grow in their knowledge of God's written Word and His will for their lives. The relationship might last for only two or three meetings, but the concept was effective in providing key initial help when persons were just starting their journey of faith.

A similar concern for helping new and veteran members be secure about the basics of the Christian faith led Carol Ellsworth to develop Growing Discipleship: Heart to Heart. "Where does a person go for help who has just come into the faith?" she asks. "We need people to come along aside to be available. You just can't force it." So Ellsworth has developed a course of study used at Redeemer Lutheran Church, Spokane, Washington, which can be done one-on-one, couple-to-couple, or in a small group of mentors and mentees.

The mentoring course begins with the core truths of the Christian faith. It then moves to the areas of priorities and goals for the Christian life, spiritual "habits of the heart" to aid Christian growth, and accountability to other Christians, and then into a natural sharing of the faith. "People are really hungering," she says. "We take so much for granted. Being 'in the Word' is a real key for spiritual growth." She uses the picture of Jesus' walk to Emmaus on the afternoon of His resurrection as an image of the kind of mentoring for which she aims. "We're walking with Jesus, holding the hand of another," she says.

Mentoring to help with spiritual growth also is an excellent tool for persons at other points in their spiritual life. Dave Kraft offers a four-hour seminar on mentoring called "Life on Life," which he has presented for the Pacific Southwest District of The Lutheran Church—Missouri

Synod, among other places. He also focuses personally on selecting Christians to mentor whom he feels have the potential and the gifts from God to be leaders in the church. "My purpose is to leave footprints in the hearts of God-hungry leaders who reproduce other leaders," he says.

Rev. Darold Reiner has used a short-term form of mentoring to help his junior high confirmation students benefit from the insights of a veteran member. The students at Trinity Lutheran Church, Kalispell, Montana, have the opportunity to request an adult member (other than their parents) to meet with them after the six midweek services during Lent. These adults who mentor are called sponsors. Reiner suggests questions about the Christian faith and life that the pairs can discuss. They talk for an hour, although some discussions have run as long as 90 minutes. After the program's first year, a feedback session involving students, mentors, and parents showed that response to the idea was overwhelmingly positive.

Mentoring is a tool by which Christians in this century can share insights from the Scriptures and help one another grow in the faith in a hostile world.

A Slice of Life

Carolyn raised her hand timidly, but Michelle encouraged her with a smile as she asked, "Do you have a question, Carolyn?" It took a few seconds for Carolyn to answer, but finally she quietly said, "What are these chapters and verses you're talking about?"

That's how Michelle and the rest of the women at the Wednesday Women Bible Study class learned that Carolyn was just beginning to explore the world of the Christian faith. Michelle knew that Carolyn had come with her brother and sister-in-law to worship at their church recently when a niece was baptized. Carolyn told Michelle she had read about the women's study group in the bulletin announcements. She wanted to learn more about the Bible. So after her second time in weekend worship, Carolyn came on her own to the class. Now she (and Michelle) were discovering how much there was for Carolyn to learn.

Michelle took her time in replying to Carolyn's question. When she answered, it was with another gentle smile and a very caring voice, so that Carolyn would not be embarrassed. "Thanks for asking, Carolyn," Michelle replied. "The Bible was written under God's inspiration by a number of authors. There are 66 books in all. To help us find our way through the Bible, someone long ago divided all but the shortest book into chapters and verses.

"If you look at the Bible you're holding, you can see that each page has words at the very top. That is the name of the book on those pages. It can be a person's name, like the first letter by John. Or it could be some other word, like Genesis, which means 'beginning,' the name for the first book of the Bible.

"Go down to the text on the page and you'll see chapter headings and then verses numbered below them. Our study group has a number of different printings and versions of the Bible, so a specific passage is not on the same page in all our Bibles. But if we identify it by book, chapter, and verse, then we can all be at the same place in the Bible."

"Thanks, Michelle," Carolyn said. "That's very helpful. I hope it wasn't a dumb question."

"No question is dumb when it comes to studying God's Word," Michelle responded, flashing one of her happy smiles. "We're glad you're here to learn with us."

Michelle meant it. After the class was over, she quietly chatted with Carolyn. "Sometimes we may refer to events or ideas from the Bible that you've not heard about, Carolyn. Would you like me to spend some time with you, to help you learn about some of what the Bible teaches?"

"Would you?" responded Carolyn, her eyes growing wide in excitement. "That would be great!" So Michelle began meeting with Carolyn every week, in addition to their being in class together. Michelle started by reading the Gospel of Mark with Carolyn. That led to a detour right away, because Carolyn had not realized that Jesus was not only a great man but also the Son of God. So Michelle paged in the Bible with Carolyn to Luke's account of Jesus' birth.

That experience led to Michelle e-mailing her pastor: "I had never read the Christmas story before to someone who didn't know it. Wow! God's power and wonderfulness just amaze me. Please pray that the Holy Spirit would continue to soften her heart and draw her closer and closer to Him. And that He would use me and the other women in our Bible class as He wills it."

That is what happened as the year progressed. Michelle continued to help Carolyn learn about Christianity, mentoring her in the basics of the Christian faith and life. Soon, Carolyn began talking about being baptized and attending the church's adult inquiry seminar, since she was considering joining the congregation. Michelle knew that her mentoring time was over. Carolyn had become her friend. Even more, Michelle thanked God that she had been used by the Holy Spirit to help someone grow in faith, learning the grace of God in Jesus and trusting in Him as her Savior.

For reflection:

1. Statistics show that persons who have little or no knowledge of the Christian faith can total as much as 40 to 60 percent of the population in most parts of the United States. How many people do you know who have no active relationship of faith with Jesus Christ?

2. Have they ever expressed an interest in learning more about your faith? If not, why not?

3. How would you respond if someone asked you a question about who Jesus is or what you believe as a Christian? What kinds of questions have you asked others about the faith?

For action:

1. If you are willing to make the effort to help mentor a new Christian for a brief time at the start of his or her time in your congregation, talk to your pastor. Tell him what kind of training you would like and why you want to help in this way.

2. Mentoring works best when specific goals and expectations are shared by the mentor and mentee. If you have an area of Christian faith or life in which you would like to be mentored, note it in the margin. If you know a Christian who could help you grow in your faith in that area, approach him or her with

your need and willingness to consider being mentored.

3. Mentoring resources are listed in the back of this book. If you have an interest in mentoring others or being trained to do so, use the list as a starting point for finding resources that could provide more information and help.

5

Mentoring to Introduce a Newcomer

Barnabas and Paul

Paul watched as Barnabas rapped on the wooden door and wondered whether they would be welcomed by the disciples of the Lord. He remembered when he had tried earlier to get into this house where the Christians in Jerusalem were staying. He so much wanted to experience fellowship with them and share the love of the Savior. In one way, Paul thought, he had earned that right.

Hadn't he risked arrest by the governor of Damascus for preaching that Jesus was the Son of God, the promised Messiah? Worse than that, his enemies had someone watching the city gates 24 hours a day, so that they might kill him if he tried to leave. He literally had to become a "basket case," being lowered to safety outside the city through an opening in the wall in a large basket. Had these Christians in Jerusalem not heard about his escape?

If not, they did remember years ago when Paul was so zealous to put the Christians into jail that he received letters of authority from the high priest to arrest followers of the Way (as they called themselves) even in faraway Damascus, a six-day journey from Jerusalem.

They had not forgotten how Paul had watched over the cloaks of those who stoned Stephen to death, with Paul's approval. So they were afraid that he had become a double agent, claiming now to be a follower of Jesus only to infiltrate the ranks of the church and achieve his greatest triumph as a persecutor. So the Christians in Jerusalem did not want Paul to become one of them.

All of this may have flashed through Paul's mind as Barnabas stood next to him at the door, rapping on the wood. But this time, the door opened and they were admitted. And things were different. For Barnabas assured the apostles and the other followers of Jesus that Paul's new faith was genuine. Instead of being a double agent, Paul was now the agent of Jesus. The risen Savior had miraculously appeared to Paul on the road to Damascus, not in a vision, but in His resurrected person.

The bright light of Jesus' appearance had not only blinded Paul for three days. It also had flooded his soul with the truth that Jesus was the promised Messiah, the Son of God as well as the Son of Man.

Barnabas told how Paul had fasted for three days, after which the Lord had sent a disciple named Ananias to restore Paul's sight and give him the Holy Spirit by the laying on of hands. Paul had been baptized. He had listened to Ananias's message from the Lord that Paul would be God's chosen instrument to preach Jesus before the Gentiles, the non-Jews. That would include suffering for the sake of Jesus and His Gospel. That suffering had already begun, with Paul's fearless preaching in Damascus and the threats against his life.

Barnabas took the side of the former persecutor and

saw that he was accepted by the Christian leaders into their community. Barnabas had become a mentor for a newcomer, who would become the apostle Paul.

For reflection:

1. Acts 9:1–31 tells the unlikely story of how the chief persecutor of the Christians became one of their leaders. How was Ananias a mentor to Paul? How did Barnabas serve in that way?

2. The Gospel not only is the "power of God for . . . salvation" (Romans 1:16). It also has the ability to change lives. When someone is called to faith in Jesus Christ, why is there a need for Christians to serve as mentors for this new believer?

3. Who were your mentors when you became part of a congregation and started to grow in your faith and life as a Christian? What did they do to help you? Is there anything you wish they had not done—or anything you wish they would have added—in their mentoring?

Exploring the Concept

Regardless of how experts organize the various activities they include under the umbrella of "mentoring," chances are good you won't find "mentoring the newcomer" listed.

Maybe that's because a variety of skills can be needed to help someone new to a group or organization. In addition, each newcomer will be different, with his or her own set of strengths on which to build and another set of areas to develop into strengths. Material focusing on mentoring newcomers approaches mentoring from the theoretical rather than the practical side. But when congregations are looking for help, usually it's practical needs motivating them, rather than the desire to implement a theoretical model.

So how do we go about mentoring newcomers to the church or our team or ministry or committee in a congregation? Barnabas provides an excellent example with his mentoring of Paul in Acts 9. Ted W. Engstrom recognizes this fact in *The Fine Art of Mentoring*, one of the earliest books to deal with mentoring from a Christian perspective. Engstrom lists five actions that were keys to Barnabas truly being a "Son of Encouragement" (the name he received from the apostles because of his caring; originally he had been called Joseph the Levite).

Those keys for mentoring Paul were being generous, learning to know people and believe in them, displaying a willingness to risk for someone whom you are mentoring, becoming excited when good happens in the lives of others, and affirming others so they grow in their life as Christians.[1]

Mentoring a newcomer highlights the caring nature of an interpersonal relationship that is key to mentoring. Even businesses realize that it's helpful to have a veteran employee mentor someone new. How much more fitting it would be for congregations to offer mentoring to persons new to their fellowship! After all, Christian congregations claim to follow in the footsteps of the early believers who were described by a pagan observer as different. "See how they love one another," he said about them. If any group has the motive and the means to help a newcomer become part of a caring group, it's a Christian church.

There are other reasons, too. Congregations, like most other organizations, operate not only by written procedures but also by unwritten rules and traditions. The unwritten traditions often are procedures that new persons have no chance to know, unless they either break the traditions (and suffer the consequences) or have a mentor to let them know what's expected.

For example, consider someone who is a newcomer and wants to be a worship service volunteer. Some congregations have an unwritten rule that women cannot serve as ushers. Even though it never is put into writing, the restriction stands. That kind of unwritten rule can be harder to change than a bylaw in the parish constitution. Or take the matter of worship clothing. I remember being the only person in a suit and tie in a new congregation aimed at parents in their 20s and 30s. Casual dress was an unwritten rule, which was never publicized or spoken in so many words. I truly felt like a newcomer when I worshiped there. It was as if I had a sign on my back that said, "I'm a newcomer. I don't know the dress code here." It was not a welcoming feeling.

That's one good reason for welcoming newcomers by mentoring. Another is to help persons find their niche in the ministries of the local body of Christ, the congregation. Mentoring can fit right into the new member welcoming process of a congregation. Signal Hill Lutheran Church, Belleville, Illinois, uses an adaptation of group and individual mentoring to help new members feel part of the congregation.

All new members attend a Bible study class focusing on what the New Testament teaches about spiritual gifts and abilities. Newcomers then are asked to assess how they believe the Holy Spirit has gifted them, based on their reading of the Scripture, their experiences, and their feedback from other people. After meeting with staff members to talk about what they have discovered, newcomers are invited to be involved in church activities that put these talents and abilities to use for the glory of God.

The next natural step is for someone, often the leader or a senior member of a team or board, to mentor them in how and why the group functions. But such mentoring can slip between the cracks. So the church has a volunteer coordinator who checks with the group leader to see what has happened with the new member, while the deacon assigned to the geographic area in which the new member lives follows up from that side. Accountability is important not only for the mentee but also for the mentor.

Some congregations focus simply on introducing a newcomer to enough people to feel "at home" and cared for. So they recruit sponsors who may do anything from inviting the new member to their Bible class to sitting with them in worship to introducing them to a certain number of members in the first three months after joining. While this is informal mentoring, it does put some structure and expectations into the responsibility of making a newcomer feel welcome.

Everyone has experienced being the new kid on the block and feeling left out at the start. While this feeling may be unavoidable, mentoring a newcomer can eliminate some of the uneasiness and help the person feel part of the group more quickly. Barnabas's mentoring of Paul led to this newcomer quickly taking up the cause of Christ by presenting the case for Jesus as the Jewish Messiah.

Paul shows that mentoring a newcomer not only improves how a new member feels about his or her place in the congregation. It also leads to more effective use of the gifts, talents, and abilities that the Holy Spirit gives to each Christian.

A Slice of Life

Ed always served behind the scenes. Although he was a top executive in a well-known local company, Ed never wanted to be president of the congregation. The most that he would consent to was being elected as vice president of the parish or chairing the board of elders.

Yet Ed (not his real name) served as an important mentor for me when I was the new pastor in the congregation. The mentoring relationship was never formalized or even stated in so many words. However, as a young pastor I grew to appreciate Ed's advice and experience and learned from it.

One Sunday morning, the sermon at the first of our two services fell flat. I was painfully aware of it. So at the water cooler in the basement afterward, I sought out Ed and asked what was wrong. Ed told me in a few pointed sentences. As soon as I heard the comments, I knew how to fix the sermon and make it much more effective in the second service.

I didn't always agree with Ed. At one meeting, the board of elders was having its monthly discussion of members not regular in worship attendance and ways to encourage them to come.

"You know," Ed said, "going to church is a good habit." I thought otherwise and said so: "That may be true, but people should come to church because they want to." It was the answer I had learned in theology classes and firmly believed.

Over the years, I learned that the question of how to encourage Christians to be in worship has more than one right answer. Ed's answer also was correct. I read how the writer to the Hebrew Christians encouraged them to have the habit of gathering regularly for worship (Hebrews 10:25). But I really gained a new appreciation for Ed's viewpoint when I came to realize that Jesus was in the habit of going off by Himself to pray (Luke 5:16).

As a young pastor, I learned not just from what Ed said but also from what he did. He chaired the funding portion of two major remodeling programs at the congregation within 10 years. Ed's style was to gather a group of church leaders, gain pledges for extra giving from them, and then find volunteers to go to the rest of the congregation members and encourage them to pledge extra offerings for the needed work.

That was pretty standard practice in congregational building programs, I knew. But after the campaign results showed that members intended to give enough extra offerings to meet the remodeling costs, nothing more was done. The three-year pledge forms weren't looked at again. No one was reminded to keep up with his or her pledge.

Ed believed that if members made their pledge with good intentions, they would carry through without being checked on. If their financial situation changed so that they couldn't complete the pledge, there was nothing the church could do about it anyway. The important part of the effort was to help members see the need for extra giving and to provide a way for them to do it.

I had been at the congregation almost 15 years when Ed died after a serious illness. As I reflect on Ed's life, I have realized that Ed was a mentor to me as a newcomer. The mentoring was informal and unstated. But it was mentoring nevertheless.

For reflection:

1. Who was a mentor for you when you were a new-comer at your church? How did he or she help you?

2. For what newcomers are you serving as a mentor in your congregation? What do you do to mentor them?

3. Rank the following activities by number to describe what you would like a mentor to do for you (1 would be most important, 2 second-most important, and so on):

   - clue me in on how things happen around here
   - hold me accountable for continuing to be faithful in worship and Bible study
   - suggest resources for my growing in the Christian faith
   - be willing to give forgiveness when I make a mistake
   - be willing to ask for forgiveness when he/she makes a mistake
   - accept me for who I am and help to see what Christ would have me become
   - gently challenge me to grow in my serving my Savior through involvement in congregational ministries

For action:

1. What does your congregation do to make newcomers feel at home? Informally ask some newcomers you know about how your congregation has helped them to feel wanted.

2. Do you know anyone who joined your congregation within the last five years but then dropped into inactivity? If so, ask that person about the kind of welcome they received when they joined. Ask what the congregation could have done to help keep them active. Share what you have learned with your pastor.

6

Mentoring to Prepare for Serving

Paul and Timothy

Timothy shook his head in amazement as he heard what Paul had in mind. His proposal that Timothy travel with the apostle was a complete shock. What an opportunity it would be to learn more about the truths of the Way, to help Paul, and to listen to him preach! Even the necessity of being circumcised to avoid trouble with the Jews did not bother him. Timothy was ready to prepare for Christian serving by assisting Paul (Acts 16:1–5).

From this point in the New Testament, Timothy becomes one of Scripture's most mentioned Christian leaders, besides the original apostles and Paul. Sometimes Timothy travels with Paul; at other times, he is with Silas. Timothy spends time with the apostle in Corinth and may have followed Paul when he was imprisoned in Rome, because Timothy is mentioned in several letters written by Paul during that time. After Paul's release, he entrusts Timothy with the pastorship of the important congregation in Ephesus. It is while Timothy is serving here that Paul twice writes to his young pastor friend.

It is apparent that Paul is continuing through correspondence what he earlier has done for Timothy in person: mentoring to prepare the young pastor for serving. Timothy is not mentioned as an apostle or an overseer in any New Testament writings. He was set aside for the work of preaching and teaching by the laying on of hands (1 Timothy 4:14). We know he was to do the work of an evangelist (2 Timothy 4:5).

If you read through these two letters to Timothy, you can see the kind of advice and instruction that Paul is giving, all with the goal of helping Timothy teach the truth about Jesus in love to the people of Ephesus. Yet Paul also reveals the caring relationship that is part of every good mentoring arrangement. Twice in the last chapter of 2 Timothy, Paul urges Timothy to come quickly before winter (2 Timothy 4:9 and 21). He asks Timothy to help him by bringing a cloak, his papyrus scrolls, and his animal skin parchments, which may have been "file copies" of his writings to the early church.

We don't know if Timothy made it to Paul in time to be with the apostle before he suffered martyrdom for the sake of the Gospel. We do know that later in his life, Timothy was imprisoned and then released (Hebrews 13:23). Nothing else is heard about him. But even that fits the kind of mentoring he received. For Timothy was mentored by Paul not to succeed him as an apostle or a writer of New Testament letters, but to serve. From what the New Testament tells us, Paul's mentoring of Timothy was successful. He became a servant.

Exploring the Concept

You've achieved your first goal: recruiting someone to

serve as a board member or Sunday school teacher or hospital visitor. But you're only halfway to the ultimate objective of that person finding satisfaction and joy in using God-given gifts to build up the body of Christ, the church. To accomplish that, someone needs to offer training to the new volunteer. Mentoring for serving is a good way to provide that help.

That mentoring can take a variety of forms. Jean Weidler sees mentoring as a good way to help new teachers feel more comfortable in education ministries of the church. "For instance," she says, "someone may have a love for children and be willing to teach, but just not know how to go about it." So mentoring can be useful in equipping persons to teach in Sunday school, midweek school, confirmation class, Bible class, vacation Bible school, or Christian day school, as Jean has done at Immanuel Lutheran School, Batavia, Illinois.

Jean has served as "the mentor next door" to new classroom teachers. Even though a beginning teacher has gone through student teaching, "that gives only a taste of what day-to-day teaching is like," Jean says. In one case, she was able to help a new second grade teacher in several ways. Before classes started, Jean mentored her in practical class procedures, as well as covering the curriculum and telling her about the incoming students, whom Jean had taught as the first grade teacher months before. "It was helping her with the 'nuts and bolts' which aren't taught in a class."

"The most important thing," Jean goes on, "was to encourage and praise her, as well as being available when she had questions. I wanted her to be confident enough to ask questions, yet be able to treat her as another professional on the staff." As the year went on, the close relationship continued, but Jean found the mentoring decreasing as the new teacher grew in experience and skill.

Many new pastors in The Lutheran Church—Missouri Synod are experiencing the benefits of PALS (Post-Seminary Applied Leaning Seminar and Support), according to its director, Rev. Dr. Bruce Hartung, St. Louis, Missouri. Regional clusters of seminary graduates meet as a small group for six days during a year with a veteran pastor. He serves as group facilitator for the program of worship, Bible study, a topic presentation, discussion of problems, and fellowship. While some might call this group mentoring—in which a mentor works with two or more mentees at the same time—Hartung prefers not to use that term. He considers mentoring, by definition, to occur between two individuals, with the mentee selecting the mentor. In the case of PALS, congregations typically pay for their young pastor to be part of the group and expect him to attend.

But the caring aspect that is a key to good mentoring is present whether or not the term is used. "These young pastors are walking into ministry," Hartung explains. "We are helping to create a group culture where they can talk indepth about personal and pastoral joys and sorrows. If they learn to do this with one another, then hopefully they will move on to being able to have 'real' relationships in the same way with lay leaders in their congregations."

One result of PALS is that pastors learn that they can help one another in what sometimes is called peer mentoring. That occurs when two persons help one another, exchanging the roles of mentor and mentee depending on what they're discussing or doing.

Several resources are available nationally to provide mentoring to congregational leaders. Joy Leadership Center, Glendale, Arizona, offers a roster of people who will mentor on specific areas of service, including strategic planning, worship planning, adult education, and youth education. These mentors can connect with mentees in person, by phone, by interactive video, or via the Internet. According to Diane Eggum of the Center staff, this mentoring "is not 'do it our way,' but looking at principles which the mentees can put to work in their own congregations."

Also using mentoring is the Pastoral Leadership Institute (PLI) as it works to train pastors in the field. Rev. Dr. Norbert Oesch explains that PLI approaches mentoring as a "personal mosaic." Instead of being mentored by only one person, mentees are encouraged to seek mentoring from a variety of experts, each one in his or her own field. Pastors who complete the four-year PLI continuing education program in advanced leadership will have been involved with 12 pastors in The Lutheran Church—Missouri Synod whose congregations have one or more "signature ministries" about which they can serve as mentors.

Whether mentoring is one-on-one or in small groups, whether it happens in person or through technological connections, if the mentor prepares the mentee for Christian serving, the goal of the relationship has been met.

A Slice of Life

"Pastor, I've been thinking that there is a way in which I would like to serve in the church." That's how the phone call from Latisha began. Pastor Gary took a deep breath before he answered. "Oh?" he responded noncommittally. "Just what did you have in mind?"

"I'd like to visit people," she replied. "I so much appreciated how you came to see me those days when I was in the hospital. And I know how much my mother looks forward to your visits in the nursing home. Is there some way I can help in those ministries?"

"I would certainly hope so," the pastor responded, more sure now of what was coming. "Let me take a week to think about this, look around for some resources, and then get back to you. In the meantime, let's both pray that God would guide whatever happens about your desire to serve in this way."

Pastor Gary was as good as his word. He began by glancing through the pastoral care books he had studied in seminary. They were helpful, but even more beneficial was a phone call to a seminary classmate now serving as a hospital chaplain in another part of the state. The chaplain told him that many congregations were using lay callers to make visits in hospitals and nursing homes, as well as to visit those recovering from hospitalization. He mentioned that the Stephen Series provided training for lay callers to deal in more depth with difficult situations. He encouraged Pastor Gary to begin mentoring Latisha in visitation ministry and mentioned several resources for reading that he thought would be helpful for the congregation to purchase for this new volunteer.

That's what the pastor did. But he went a step further. He asked the board of elders if any of them might be interested in also being trained for hospital and shut-in visitation. Chris responded that he had often thought about the possibility of serving in that way but never had thought it would be possible. He became Pastor Gary's second volunteer.

That was good for a number of reasons. One was very practical. Pastor Gary, in mentoring or other ministry, made it a practice never to be alone with a woman in his office or in the car. This prevented possible suspicions or criticisms. Chris's volunteering meant that there would be three people present in the drives to the hospitals and the nursing homes. But a second good reason for three of them being together was that it equalized the relationship dynamics. While Pastor Gary was the mentor, both Latisha and Chris were Christians with a lot of caring and good skills in listening.

At first this meant that both mentees asked a lot of questions after pairing off with the pastor on their calls. Having three of them involved seemed to stimulate the kind of growth by questioning that Pastor Gary enjoyed moderating. But as they read the books and learned to do reports on what had occurred during their visits, their comments grew more insightful. Pastor Gary felt that he also was learning from the experience. He began to see new possibilities for his visitation ministry. As Latisha and Chris came nearer to making visits on their own, their excitement grew.

Pastor Gary found that he was excited, too. He had heard about a congregation with lay visitors that had put the expectations of such calling into writing, so he did the same. He and his mentees talked about how often they wanted to visit and how long a commitment they wished to make. They discussed what would be most helpful for keeping the communication channels open between the mentees and Pastor Gary, so that a visitor would not be caught off-guard by a new development in the life of a person since the visitor's last call.

Then came the week for the first calls by Latisha and Chris. Pastor Gary felt a special joy in his heart as he read their reports. He knew that they were doing well in their serving. In some situations they even had easier access than he to the feelings and condition of the patient, because of their personal histories. And he knew that their serving in the visitation ministry freed him to do other work that only a pastor could do. But his main source of satisfaction was that other members of the congregation were using their gifts and abilities for serving.

For reflection:

1. Have you ever begun serving in the church simply because you were interested in a particular area of service, before anyone asked?

2. Why do you think Pastor Gary was noncommittal when he received Latisha's phone call? Why are church professionals sometimes wary of "letting go" in the areas in which they serve?

3. Do you know of situations in which someone has volunteered for ministry in a certain area and fallen flat on his or her face? What were the consequences for ministry? How does mentoring guard against people failing because they are unprepared or unqualified?

4. Do you know of situations in which a volunteer has

served so well that the ministry is expanded? Was mentoring involved? Could it be now?

For action:

Make a list of the various ways in which people serve in your congregation. Then list the ways in which only the professionals on your staff currently serve. Could some of those areas of "professionals only" serving be opened to members? How? What would be the reaction of the professionals if they were asked to share or give up this area of ministry? Would this be good or bad for the congregation?

7

Risks and Benefits
of Mentoring

Demas and Luke

Three times they are mentioned in the same breath by the apostle Paul. Twice they represent the joy of persons who served alongside Paul and were mentored by him. But their final mention contrasts Demas, who "has deserted me," with Luke: "Only Luke is with me" (2 Timothy 4:10–11).

Even a mentor of Christians as great as the apostle Paul knew from bitter experience that not all mentoring succeeds. Yet that did not stop him from working with as many mentees as possible, all for the sake of the Gospel.

Paul initially describes Demas as a fellow worker or laborer for the Lord Jesus. Few Christians in the New Testament were able to say that about themselves. If the apostle Paul was the greatest missionary of the early church, then Demas had the opportunity to be mentored by the best. The fact that Paul mentions him in both his letters to the Colossians and to Philemon tells us something about how important Demas was to Paul.

Yet somewhere, somehow, something went wrong. By the time Paul writes his final New Testament epistle, the

Second Letter to Timothy, Paul bemoans the fact that he is almost all alone. Demas has deserted him, the apostle writes, and gone to Thessalonica "because he loved this world" (2 Timothy 4:10).

There's a strong contrast that stands out in the original text of Paul's words. We could translate that Demas was in love with "the 'now' world." Awkward as that is in English, it gives us Paul's perspective that there is so much more in life than what is going on in the present time. How sad that Demas traded that gift for the passing pleasures of what the world has to offer "now."

Demas' love for "what's happening now" contrasts with the benefits of Paul's mentoring of Luke, whom he calls the "beloved physician." If Demas is an example of grace refused, Luke is a shining light of the amazing grace of God working in the heart of someone used in a special way for the Lord's work.

We don't know that because of what Luke tells us about himself. We don't even know where he was born or received his medical training or how he came to be with Paul. He is the author of the two-volume New Testament work of the Gospel of Luke and the Acts of the Apostles. That leads scholars to guess that he joined Paul on his second missionary journey at the seaport of Troas, from which Paul and his companions sailed to bring the Gospel to Europe for the first recorded time. That assumption arises because Luke says "we" sailed to Macedonia.

Luke stays very much in the background of what he reports, except for the occasional "we" in the history recorded in Acts. Luke is mentioned by the apostle to the Gentiles, so it would seem that he was with Paul quite often during the latter part of the apostle's life and helped him when no one else was there (2 Timothy 4:11).

That was a benefit of mentoring that Paul probably had not expected. It is a good reminder that mentors can be enriched by their mentoring just as mentees are, although in different ways.

We also benefit from Luke's being mentored by Paul. What would our Christian faith and life be like without the beautiful Christmas story (Luke 2)? Think of the pointed parables showing how Jesus has come for those who are lost (Luke 15). Then there is the history of the early Christian church (in the Acts of the Apostles), showing how the Holy Spirit worked through ordinary people like us to spread the Good News about Jesus.

If Demas shows us the risk of mentoring and being disappointed, Luke reminds us that God uses mentoring as a tool in the ministry He plans for His people to do. In this case, the benefits outweigh the risks of failing.

For reflection:

1. Do you know someone who was mentored by a Christian leader, yet like Demas turned away from the faith? What was the reason in the situation you know about?

2. Think about a Christian leader who mentored you. Do you know who that person's mentor was? If we benefit from Paul's mentoring of Luke, how do you benefit from your mentor first being mentored by another?

3. Have you ever helped another Christian, only to be disappointed when that person turned his or her back on the Christian church and its faith? How did that

affect your willingness to mentor others at the time? How do you feel about it now?

4. Are you aware of persons who consider you their mentor, even though you never thought of what you did for them in that way? How was your mentoring like that of Paul with Luke?

5. How is the grace of God involved in all mentoring, whether it seems to be a failure or success at the end?

Exploring the Concept

Rev. Ed Lang enjoys mentoring so much that he was hoping to continue doing it after he retired. Lang was a missions executive with the Missouri District of The Lutheran Church—Missouri Synod. His work included mentoring ten pastors in Missouri—six involving ethnic ministries (Hispanic, Vietnamese, Messianic Jewish, and Chinese) and four planting new Anglo churches in metropolitan areas of the state.

Why did his church organization set up Lang as a mentor for these mission planters? He answers that question by saying that book learning is fine, but there just are some aspects of beginning a mission congregation that can be communicated best by someone who has experience and training.

Lang prepared for that mentoring by attending the Mission Planters Institute of the parent church body. He was trained in coaching young pastors, learning how to mentor them and what to look for in choosing pastor mentees (not everyone qualifies to be mentored).

His mentoring included the expectation that the

mentees would develop a plan including their vision for their congregation, values on which this was based, a ministry plan, and a timetable for carrying out that ministry. They in turn would benefit in their regular sessions from a time of prayer, having Lang serve as a sounding board, and, "since they were plowing new ground," as Lang says, having an experienced pastor help explore their options and anticipate the results of each of them.

"This is bold, venturesome stuff," Lang says with a smile. "We're working in areas and in ways the church hasn't tried in our district before."

Usually his contacts with the new pastors continued for 12 to 18 months. "You can tell when they are ready to assume responsibility for their ministry, based on the maturity of the new mission," Lang says.

Although he was scheduled to retire at the end of Year 2000, Lang was saying a year earlier that he would like to keep on mentoring in some way. He admitted that there are risks in mentoring, especially "losing patience" when mentees aren't willing to listen. But Lang saw several benefits for mentors. First, some people in their jobs do not have a lot of interaction with other people. Mentoring provides one-to-one contact with real people with real needs. Second, when you mentor someone, Lang says, "you rejoice and cry with them, you bond, you celebrate their victories."

After several years of mentoring young pastors, Lang feels that pastors (including those he has mentored) would do well to consider mentoring their lay leaders. Whether this will work depends, he feels, partially on the personality of the pastor. Lang explains that "the pastor would have to give up part of the decision-making process" if he chooses to mentor others.

But Lang obviously feels the risks of mentoring are worth the benefits. Why else would he be willing to keep on with it, after he has retired?

Mentoring experts probably would agree with Ed Lang about the benefits he lists. But some would also alert us to risks that can arise—not just for the mentor, but also for the mentee. Susan Ford Wiltshire talks about four dangers of mentoring. These can include the mentee trying to be an unthinking duplicate of the mentor, a mentor-mentee relationship being awkward for both persons, a mentor abusing his authority, and even a mentor sexually exploiting the mentee.[1] Some of those risks make others look tame by comparison.

Bill Catlette and Richard Hadden write about how American retailers benefit when they employ the coaching form of mentoring for their employees. Mentors help their mentees become committed, realize that they are cared about, and help them find the tools, the trust, and the training to do their jobs well.[2]

One potential pitfall to avoid, according to Christian mentoring expert Dr. J. Robert Clinton, is nepotism—rewarding someone because you mentor them, not because they have earned the reward.[3] He also notes that mentors make themselves vulnerable to the gaze of their mentees, who may, as a result, learn how *not* to do things that reflect flaws in the mentor's abilities or style.[4] If a person doesn't want someone else to see the not-so-perfect aspects of his life, staying away from mentoring probably is a good decision.

Yet mentoring has the potential, at its best, to be what Dr. Clinton calls it: "a relational experience through which one person empowers another by sharing God-given resources."[5] With that kind of relationship as the result, many Christian leaders think mentoring is worth the risks.

A Slice of Life

Pastor George was intrigued when Mory and Denise phoned him for an appointment to see whether he would perform their wedding. Mory came from a Roman Catholic background. He had been previously married and because of that could not be married in his former church. Denise had been active in the Baptist church while growing up and also was divorced after a first marriage. The priest at Mory's home parish down the street recommended the neighboring Lutheran minister, Pastor George, as someone with whom the couple might be comfortable performing the marriage ceremony.

Pastor George liked the honesty of Mory and Denise, as well as their willingness to attend his adult inquiry class. That was standard procedure in his congregation whenever nonmember couples were married there. The pastor appreciated the questions the couple raised during the class sessions and was not surprised when they decided to join the church.

Both came regularly to worship, were active participants in Bible class, and soon were invited to assume leadership positions. Mory was willing to serve as an usher. But he balked when he learned ushers were expected to wear a suit and tie when ushering. Denise served on the board for youth ministry but found it difficult to work with teenagers who didn't seem very motivated to be involved in church activities.

Mory used Pastor George as an informal mentor while his spiritual search continued. Once or twice a month the minister would spend between 30 and 60 minutes on the phone with Mory, trying to guide him into understanding a Lutheran approach to a variety of issues in response to his questioning.

In the meantime, Denise became pregnant with a baby who was a high medical risk. She ended up in a hospital an hour's drive away during the last weeks of the pregnancy. Pastor George was faithful in visiting her, as were other members of the congregation in expressing their caring. Denise and the baby boy both pulled through the difficult birth, and Mory and Denise were overjoyed.

A few years later a baby girl came along. As Mory and Denise struggled with the challenges of parenting while both worked full-time jobs, their commitment to the church seemed to wane. The family was in worship less and less often. Pastor George tried to find ways to involve the couple in short-term serving, but he wasn't really successful.

He wasn't all that surprised when he met Denise in the local supermarket and she told him the family had started attending a growing independent evangelical church. "Mory feels that the Lutheran church is just too much like his old church, the Roman Catholic parish," she explained. "And at your church (Pastor George winced as she said the words) we never heard anything about making a decision for Jesus Christ and yielding our lives so that we might receive the abundant life. We haven't taken up membership there yet, but I don't think we'll be back."

Her words came true. The independent congregation was the first of a number of stops on the church shopping journey that the family made in the next several years. But the family never came back to the congregation where Pastor George had served as a mentor during a crucial time in their lives.

For reflection:

1. Should mentors expect something in return when they take the time, energy, and effort to help a spiritually searching person? Why?

2. Pastor George experienced pain when a person in whom he had invested himself as a mentor eventually used those skills in another Christian congregation. What would you say to him after hearing his story?

3. What benefits for Pastor George and his congregation can you find in this story?

4. You can't mentor someone without taking risks. What other risks can you think of, besides the person using the skills gained in a way that the mentor didn't intend?

5. Which benefits of mentoring from a Christian perspective make it worth the risk of someone abusing the effort you invest in mentoring him or her?

For action:

1. If someone has disappointed you in a mentoring relationship, what steps can you take to restore that rela-

tionship? List them in the margin. Then pray for
God's guidance as you seek His will in this matter and
follow it.

2. If you have disappointed someone in a mentoring
   relationship, read #1 and follow the steps there.

8

Mentoring When It Gets Bumpy

Paul and John Mark

What do you do when someone who has disappointed you asks for a second chance? Do you remember the pain of when you were hurt? Do you recall your mother teaching you, "First time, shame on you. Second time, shame on me"? Or do you base your reaction on the fact that Christianity has been called "the religion of the second chance"?

The apostle Paul was faced with such a decision in his ministry. The story begins when Paul sets off on his first missionary journey, with Barnabas as his partner. Barnabas brings his cousin John Mark along as a helper (Acts 13:5). Scripture doesn't use the word, but it sounds like the younger man is serving as an apprentice to the two apostles.

But things don't work out. After they sail from Cyprus to the southern coast of modern-day Turkey, John Mark leaves. No one knows exactly why. Some speculate that John Mark became homesick. Others note that in Acts 12:25, when the young man goes with the apostles from Jerusalem to Antioch, Barnabas is named first, perhaps indicating he was leader. However, when Luke records that the missionary group sails to Turkey, Paul is named first (Acts 13:13). Maybe John Mark didn't like the fact that his cousin no longer was in charge. Whatever the reason, John Mark went home.

Paul doesn't forget. When Paul later invites Barnabas to take a second missionary trip with him to encourage the churches they had planted together on the first journey, Barnabas suggests that John Mark accompany them. But Paul disagrees sharply, Luke notes, because Mark "had deserted them in Pamphylia and had not continued with them in the work" (Acts 15:38).

The disagreement is so strong that pair splits. Barnabas goes with Mark to Cyprus (Barnabas's home island), and Paul chooses Silas to travel with him. That would seem to be the end of the mentoring of Mark by Paul. In fact, Scripture suggests that eventually Mark began to work with Peter (1 Peter 5:13). The early church leader Papias (about A.D. 140) writes that Peter's preaching is the main source of the Second Gospel, authored by Mark.

Yet Paul and Mark's relationship was not finished. At one point, Paul writes to Christians who live near Colossae, the area where Mark had left Paul years earlier. He says that Mark sends his greetings. "You have received instructions about him," the apostle continues. "If he comes to you, welcome him" (Colossians 4:10). Scholars estimate this to be about 12 years after Barnabas and Paul had parted ways over Mark. Even more interesting is a comment by Paul five years after these words in Colossians. Paul writes in his final New Testament letter that he wants Timothy to bring Mark along to visit Paul, because Mark "is helpful to me in my ministry" (2 Timothy 4:11).

What happened? We don't know any details. But judging from the change in Paul's attitude, we can be certain that he took his own inspired words to the Ephesians to heart: "Be kind and compassionate to one another, forgiving each other, just as in Christ God forgave you" (Ephesians 4:32). Certainly Mark also was involved, seeking to restore the relationship with his one-time mentor and admitting any mistakes he had made or sins he had done against Paul.

Even in the best of mentoring relationships, disagreements can occur. Both persons involved are imperfect sinners. Paul's relationship with John Mark shows us that forgiveness—requested and given—is an essential part of the Christian faith and certainly a key to any mentoring relationship between Christians.

For reflection:

1. Mentors are chosen because they have something to give to the mentee. An admiring mentee can put the mentor on a pedestal. How is this dangerous in a relationship involving two humans?

2. What steps can be taken to avoid either the mentor or the mentee disappointing each other? What can a Christian mentor do to facilitate this? What is needed for the mentee to be able to be honest with the mentor when he or she is disappointed?

3. What difference can it make in a mentor-mentee relationship if both are Christians? How do Paul's words about "speaking the truth in love" (Ephesians 4:15) and "forgiving each other" (Ephesians 4:32) enter in?

4. What do Paul's final words about Mark indicate can happen in a relationship after it is restored through forgiveness requested and given?

Exploring the Concept

Mentoring doesn't always work out the way we intend. That may sound like a good reason to avoid mentoring in the first place, but it's not. Realizing that there will be bumps along the way in mentoring simply reflects the fact that any human relationship will involve two or more sinful human beings. A good mentoring relationship will not only reflect God's grace in the interactions between the persons involved; it also will use that grace to get over the bumps along the way through the gifts of requesting and receiving forgiveness.

Mentoring can involve some rockiness in a relationship because mentoring includes possessing power and also challenging the mentee, as Jerry Kosberg points out in his excellent training video, "Mentoring: Sharing the Journey." Power is involved because mentors by their very nature will make judgments about what mentees need to learn and their progress in that growing. As Kosberg notes, many mentors are uneasy with the power that they hold in the relationship.[1] It is so much easier to affirm mentees for doing well than to use the power to hold them accountable. Yet accountability to the mentor is an essential part of mentoring. Otherwise, the mentee may be tempted not to follow through on the goals agreed upon with the mentor.

A mentor is perhaps even more likely to stir feelings of resentment by challenging a mentee to grow. There's a parallel here with the power issue, because challenging a mentee to stretch and grow often means change, which is not always appreciated by a mentee. Like affirmation, support often is a natural and enjoyable aspect of mentoring. But challenging the mentee also is necessary, whether it means assigning various tasks (reading a book, trying a new technique in a difficult situation, looking at a task from a different angle) or working to set higher standards or holding a person to these standards. Kosberg notes that holding a mentee to standards is never easy, but if the relationship has been set up in the right way, the mentee will agree that the mentor has the responsibility to do so.[2]

In these and other aspects of mentoring, the mentee may become upset with the mentor and lash out in anger. Less frequently, veteran mentors may have to admit that they have used mentoring relationships primarily for their own advantage, rather than to help mentees grow. When the self-centeredness with which we all are born rears its ugly, sinful head, then the grace of God in Jesus Christ, crucified for our sins and risen for our salvation, is needed. We need to ask for forgiveness. The Bible shows how this is done.

"Confess your sins to each other" (James 5:16). Paul urges us to be forgiving to one another, "just as in Christ God forgave you" (Ephesians 4:32). As usual, Paul in a few words provides the key, pointing us back to the forgiveness we ourselves have received first. Whether we are being mentored or doing the mentoring, we can only request or receive forgiveness from the other person because God has first forgiven us. We have that assurance in John's First Letter: "if we confess our sins, He is faithful and just and will forgive us our sins" (1 John 1:9).

Declaring God's grace and love to another Christian is part of what the Lutheran doctrinal statements are talking about when they mention the priesthood of all believers. One of the ways in which God's Good News of salvation, the Gospel, is shared is through "the mutual conversation and consolation" of brothers and sisters in Christ, as the Smalcald Articles state.

There is one further step we can take. When a sin bothers us so that we "know and feel [it] in our hearts," Martin Luther encourages Christians, in the Small Catechism, to go to their pastor for private confession and absolution. This involves confessing to the pastor especially those sins that trouble us and hearing him speak the Word of God, who forgives sins.

Martin Luther found the use of a "father confessor" essential to his spiritual life. Johann von Staupitz, Luther's superior in the Augustinian order and at Wittenberg University, served in that role for Luther in addition to mentoring Luther during the first critical years of the Reformation. Luther was later to write in his Large Catechism that when he urged people to go to confession, he simply was urging them to live out their Christian life.

When mentoring is part of what those in a church do for one another, requesting and receiving forgiveness will be part of what happens.

A Slice of Life

Joe felt deeply hurt. He had been mentoring Phil as a member of the board for outreach for more than half a year. Because Phil had a special interest in making follow-up calls on people who had worshiped in their church, Joe was willing to invest time and effort in Phil's growth as an evangelizing Christian.

They agreed upon a mentor-mentee relationship even though Joe really didn't need another commitment to squeeze into his agenda. As chairperson of the board, Joe not only worked with the pastor to prepare the agenda for the monthly meeting. He also was involved in the monthly council meetings at the church, speaking up for an outreach mindset in the entire ministry of the church and reporting on what the board for outreach was planning. But Joe had prayed about Phil's interest and really believed that he needed to respond to Phil's request.

Those first six months had been a joy. The pastor had suggested several books on evangelism that Joe and Phil could read and discuss. Joe delighted in finding someone else whose heart burned with a concern for those who were lost without Christ. Sometimes it was hard to squeeze in the time for their monthly meeting as well as the night each month when they visited in the community, but Joe felt it was worthwhile. After all, hadn't the Lord himself sent out the 70 disciples two-by-two to spread the Good News of salvation?

And Phil was a quick study in how to share the Gospel. He was not pushy, but not wishy-washy either. He had learned to listen well and to respond appropriately with "his story," which led into "the story" of Jesus and what He had done for the world. Joe felt that the mentoring relationship had enriched himself, not just Phil.

That's why Joe was stunned when Phil publicly criticized a proposal of Joe's at a board for outreach meeting. Joe had wanted to buy advertising in the local newspaper for Easter worship at their congregation. He knew it would stretch the publicity budget of the board to the limit and not allow for any other ads during the rest of the year. But he thought a big, splashy advertisement would be worth the money. He had agreed at the last meeting to look into the best way to "get the word out" about the services and report on it.

"I think that's way overpriced," Phil said bluntly after Joe's presentation. "I've found out that we can get reduced rates for commercials on the local access cable TV channel for a much lower cost. I had lunch with the producer several weeks ago, and he mentioned that possibility to me. With my plan, we can even afford to advertise on the cable channel again right before Christmas." Phil was enthused about his plan, and so were the rest of the board members. They didn't even discuss Joe's option, but went right ahead and voted to go with advertising on cable TV.

To make matters worse, the pastor was sitting in on this meeting, since it was his turn to be with the outreach board in his rotation of visiting boards that met at the same time. Joe felt particularly embarrassed. He could feel his face turning a bright red, and he hurried through the rest of the meeting, then left the church with some abrupt goodbyes. Fortunately, he didn't have to face Phil, who was happily explaining the details of his plan to several board members who had volunteered to work with him on the project.

Joe shared his feelings with his wife, Sally, when he got home. She listened to him vent his disappointment, frustration, and anger. He didn't feel much like praying, but he got through the words that he and Sally prayed together each night before they went to sleep. It was not a good night's sleep, for he tossed and turned.

The next morning, Joe tried to put the episode with Phil at the church meeting out of his mind. If he just didn't think about it, things seemed better. That worked for several days. But then on the third morning after the meeting, Joe's Bible reading in his daily devotions was from the 18th chapter of Matthew's Gospel. As he read verses 21 and 22, Joe felt that Jesus was speaking straight to him: "Then Peter came to Jesus and asked, 'Lord, how many times shall I forgive my brother when he sins against me? Up to seven times?' Jesus answered, 'I tell you, not seven times, but seventy-seven times.'"

Joe knew these words of Jesus were for him, too. He realized what he had to do and placed his feelings and need for forgiveness himself into the Lord's hands in prayer. His trip to work that morning was the best it had been since the day of the church meeting.

That night, Joe phoned Phil. "I need to come over and talk with you," he said. Phil had an obligation, but they set a meeting for the next evening at Phil's house. After prayer for God's guidance, Joe began by telling Phil how much he had felt undercut by Phil's proposal at the board meeting. "It wasn't the fact that you had come up with a better idea," he explained. "What got under my skin was that you didn't give me a heads-up on your proposal. I felt you at least owed me the courtesy, not only as the chairperson but also as your mentor, to let me know beforehand what you would propose. I felt that you really made me look stupid.

"But I've been praying about it all and I've asked the Lord for forgiveness because of my feelings," Joe said.

"Phil, I need to ask you to forgive me, too."

"That's no problem," Phil responded. "But I need to ask your forgiveness also. I had no idea that you felt so strongly about what happened. I knew that I hadn't told you about the TV commercials idea, but I didn't realize it might seem that I was undercutting your idea of advertising in the newspaper. I could see you were upset. Yet I was so enthused that I didn't stop to find out why you were bothered. Now I can see why you felt the way you did.

"Joe, I'm sorry for any hurt or pain that I've caused you," Phil continued. "I need your forgiveness also. I know that God gives it to me, but I need it from you, too. Do you forgive me for my thoughtlessness?"

"Of course," Phil responded. "I realize now that you weren't intentionally trying to embarrass me. And if a mentor and his mentee can't forgive each other and move on, that relationship probably is not worth all that much. Let's pray about it." And they did.

For reflection:

1. Has another person with whom you have worked closely ever caused you to feel hurt?

   What did you do about it?

2. Have you ever had to apologize and ask forgiveness for bringing hurt to another Christian?

3. What was the hardest part of seeking someone else's forgiveness? What was the best part of the experience?

For action:

1. Identify those areas of mentoring that are the most

likely to lead to disagreements and the need for mentors or mentees to ask for forgiveness.

2. Read through the agreements for any mentoring relationships in which you are involved to see what they say about steps to take when there is a disagreement or one person feels another has sinned against him.

3. Ask your pastor about private confession and absolution and how a person desiring this gift from God can receive it through the pastor.

9

Using Mentoring in the Congregation

In some ways, the goal of this chapter already has been achieved in previous chapters. We've looked at seven examples of mentoring from the Scriptures. In applying these to modern life, we have encountered a number of ways in which congregations use mentoring as a tool for ministry.

But the list doesn't stop there. Creative leaders who seek to move the church of Jesus Christ forward in its mission keep on coming up with new ways or reviving old ways to use mentoring. Rev. Roger Sonnenberg of Our Savior Lutheran Church, Arcadia, California, believes that mentoring is a way of equipping Christians for serving that should be used throughout the whole congregation. In addition to married couples mentoring newlyweds in his congregation (chapter 2), Sonnenberg uses mentoring in a variety of other ways.

Children in his congregation often live hundreds of miles from their grandparents. So the congregation lines up "adopted" grandparents, who function in the same way as biological grandparents. They pray for their adopted grandchild, observe birthdays and other special dates, and can do activities with them, including attending their sports events. New parents are mentored by veteran parents. Single moms have an older single parent as a mentor. Confirmation students have adults who serve as mentors, as do high school students. From Sonnenberg's viewpoint, mentoring is a way for Christians to care for one another and help them serve.

Concordia Lutheran Church, Kirkwood, Missouri, used an intentional mentoring relationship a number of years ago when its senior pastor was about to retire. After the new pastor accepted the call of the congregation, he served as "pastor elect" for six months, being mentored by the outgoing minister about the congregation and community. This enabled the new pastor to learn much about the congregation from his mentor, who intentionally eased himself out of the picture in a gradual transition to the new senior pastor.

A Family Ministry Consultants Forum in November 1999, conducted by Leadership Network, included a focus on high-maintenance families, who seem to move from one crisis to another in their lives. Participants recommended setting up a family mentoring system in the congregation, so that a healthy family that had overcome a similar problem could mentor a family that was struggling. Also suggested was the use of retired persons, who often have more discretionary time, as well as experience, to share with younger families in a mentoring relationship.[1]

Mentoring also can be used as an outreach tool. The National Mentoring Working Group has published a mentor training curriculum to help organizations set up mentoring programs for youth.[2] A number of inner city congregations conduct after-school tutoring programs, which provide mentoring by using the one-on-one model. Some congregations have offered English as Second Language (ESL) programs, ministering to immigrants in that way.

The National Mentoring Partnership provides detailed help for setting up a church-based mentoring program for children at risk, ranging from organizing to training mentors to recruiting participants.[3] A variety of activities can be carried out using mentors to relate to youth who need their concern.

Such efforts show that mentoring need not be limited to serving in the congregation. As people called to be lights for Jesus Christ to the world, Christians can use mentoring as a tool in serving the community. If mentoring is defined as one Christian helping another to grow in using God-given gifts, then the sky is the limit (literally) to how mentoring can be a tool for ministry.

Some suggestions

Mentoring doesn't always go smoothly or achieve its goals. While that's to be expected because the persons involved are human and therefore sinful, some suggestions from people who have been involved in mentoring can be helpful.

- Mentoring needs to match persons who would get along well if they weren't in a mentoring relationship. If you don't like your mentor or mentee, the job just became twice as hard.

- Most often, mentoring works best if the persons involved are of the same gender. While a woman can mentor a man and a man can mentor a woman, the dynamics involved in male-female relationships can get in the way of learning.

- All mentoring is not the same. Dr. J. Robert Clinton identifies three types of mentoring: intensive (discipling, spiritual guiding, and coaching), occasional (counseling, teaching, and sponsoring), and passive (modeling, of both contemporary people and heroes from history).[4]

- While most mentoring is one-on-one, group mentoring can serve more people and can allow peer mentoring as well as the traditional mentor-mentee model. Concordia Publishing House, St. Louis, Missouri, found that its management mentoring groups functioned well with the following rules: (1) all participants function as equals; (2) the group gathers for personal and professional growth; (3) everything said in the meeting is confidential. CPH officials said such groups "function best when they help participants see meaning in and learn from experiences they share together."[5]

- "So much mentoring material is aimed at white-collar people. But we have blue-collar folk sitting in the pews," says Rev. Mike Coppersmith, pastor of Our Savior Community Lutheran Church, Palm Springs, California. Mentoring needs to be tailored to meet the attitudes, interests, and abilities of both the mentor and mentee.

- Mentoring not only has a beginning. It also ends. A typical history of a mentoring relationship involves a honeymoon, growth, maturity, decline, and closure.[6] A mentoring relationship should include a date for assessment, at which time the mentor or mentee can end the arrangement without feeling embarrassed.

• Mentoring at its best involves being mentored by someone, being a mentor to someone else, and having your peers do cooperative mentoring with you, exchanging the roles of mentor and mentee with you depending on the subject involved.

Not the End, but the Beginning

These words conclude the final chapter of this book, but they are not the end. Beyond them in these pages lies a beginning. It's the resource section, which identifies books, articles, a video, Web sites, and persons who can provide more information about mentoring as a tool for ministry. With their help, mentoring can become an important part of your life as a Christian and enrich the life of your congregation as part of the body of Christ, seeking to share the Good News of Jesus Christ, the Savior.

Notes

Special thanks are due to Signal Hill Lutheran Church, Belleville, Illinois, which granted me a three months' sabbatical to write this book.

Thanks also to the following persons who were willing to be interviewed:

Rev. Dr. J. Arthur Cox, Bradford, PA

Rev. Dennis Conrad, Orchard Park, NY

Diane Eggum, Glendale, AZ

Carol Ellsworth, Spokane, WA

Rev. Dr. Bruce Hartung, St. Louis, MO

David Kraft, Palm Springs, CA

Rev. Ed Lang, St. Louis, MO

Rev. Peter Mueller, Ellisville, MO

Rev. Dr. Norbert Oesch, Orange, CA

Rev. Darold Reiner, Kalispell, MT

Rev. Roger Sonnenberg, Arcadia, CA

Jean Weidler, Batavia, IL

Chapter 1

1 J. Robert Clinton, "Mentoring: Developing Leaders through Empowering Relationships," lecture at Calvin Seminary, Grand Rapids, Mich., Sept. 1998. (Altadena, CA: Barnabas Publishers), 3–4.

2 Clinton, 6.

3 Matt M. Starcevich, "Coach, Mentor: Is There a Difference?" article on World Wide Web site of Center for Coaching and Mentoring, June 21, 1999.

4 Starcevich.

5 Gordon F. Shea, *Mentoring: A Practical Guide,* rev. ed. (Menlo Park, CA: Crisp Publications, Inc., 1997), 15.

6 U.S. Coast Guard, "How to Be an Effective Mentor," article on World Wide Web site of Mentoring Program of U.S. Coast Guard, June 1998.

7   U.S. Coast Guard, "Five Essentials to Successful Mentoring Connections," article on World Wide Web site of Mentoring Program of U.S. Coast Guard, June 1998.

8   Clinton, 10–11.

Chapter 5

1   Ted W. Engstrom with Norman B. Rohrer, *The Fine Art of Mentoring: Passing On to Others What God Has Given You* (Brentwood, TN: Wolgemuth & Hyatt, Publishers, Inc., 1998), 10–11.

Chapter 7

1   Susan Ford Wiltshire, *Athena's Disguises: Mentors in Everyday Life* (Louisville: Westminster John Knox Press, 1998), 107–113.

2   Bill Catlette and Richard Hadden, "Coaching and *Contented Cows,*" article on World Wide Web site of Center for Coaching and Mentoring, June 19, 1999.

3   J. Robert Clinton and Paul D. Stanley, *Connecting: The Mentoring Relationships You Need to Succeed in Life* (Colorado Springs: Navpress, 1992), 127.

4   Clinton and Stanley, 141.

5   Clinton and Stanley, 12.

Chapter 8

1   Jerry Kosberg, "Mentoring: Sharing the Journey," study guide (St. Louis: Lutheran Church—Missouri Synod, Department of Leadership Ministry, 1995), 16.

2   Kosberg, 22–23.

Chapter 9

1   "The Continuing Report of the Family Ministries Consultants Forum," *Church Champions Update*, e-mail newsletter from Leadership Network, Feb. 18, 2000.

2   "The Mentor Training Curriculum," National Mentoring Partnership and United Way of America (United Way of America, undated).

3 "Church-Based Mentoring: A Program Manual for Mentoring Ministries," Church Mentoring Network, facilitated by United Way of Southeastern Pennsylvania's Volunteer Centers and Philadelphia One to One, 1994.

4 Clinton and Stanley, 41.

5 George J. Oehlert, "Mentoring: An Investment in the Future of Your Ministry," *Christian Management Report*, January/February 2000, 39.

6 "The Mentor Training Curriculum," reprint of "Values and the Match Life Cycle," Big Brothers/Big Sisters of America, Values Clarification Seminar, August 1990, 20.

References Cited

Catlette, Bill, and Richard Hadden. "Coaching and *Contented Cows*." Article on World Wide Web site of Center for Coaching and Mentoring, June 19, 1999.

"Church-Based Mentoring: A Program Manual for Mentoring Ministries." Church Mentoring Network, facilitated by United Way of Southeastern Pennsylvania's Volunteer Centers and Philadelphia One to One, 1994.

Clinton, J. Robert, and Paul D. Stanley. *Connecting: The Mentoring Relationship You Need to Succeed in Life*. Colorado Springs: Navpress, 1992.

Clinton, J. Robert. "Mentoring: Developing Leaders through Empowering Relationships," lecture at Calvin Seminary, Grand Rapids, Mich., September, 1997. Altadena, CA: Barnabas Publishers.

"The Continuing Report of the Family Ministries Consultants Forum." *Church Champions Update*, e-mail newsletter from Leadership Network, Feb. 18, 2000.

Engstrom, Ted W., with Norman B. Rohrer. *The Fine Art of Mentoring: Passing On to Others What God Has Given You*. Brentwood, TN: Wolgemuth & Hyatt, Publishers, Inc., 1989.

Kosberg, Jerry M. "Mentoring: Sharing the Journey" (videotape and study guide for eight-session course on mentoring). St. Louis: Lutheran Church—Missouri Synod, Department of Leadership Ministry, 1995. CPH order no. S02503.

"The Mentor Training Curriculum," National Mentoring Partnership and United Way of America (United Way of America, undated).

Oehlert, George J. "Mentoring: An Investment in the Future of Your Ministry." *Christian Management Report,* January/February 2000, 37–39.

Shea, Gordon F. *Mentoring: A Practical Guide.* Revised Edition. Menlo Park: Crisp Publications, Inc., 1997.

Starcevich, Matt. M. "Coach, Mentor: Is There a Difference?" Article on World Wide Web site of Center for Coaching and Mentoring, June 21, 1999.

U.S. Coast Guard. "Five Essentials to Successful Mentoring Connections." Article on World Wide Web site of Mentoring Program of Coast Guard, June 1998.

U.S. Coast Guard. "How to Be an Effective Mentor." Article on World Wide Web site of Mentoring Program of Coast Guard, June 1998.

Wiltshire, Susan Ford. *Athena's Disguises: Mentors in Everyday Life.* Louisville: Westminster John Knox Press, 1998.

Additional Resources

Barnabas Publishers, 2175 N. Holliston Ave., Altadena, CA 91001, offers a number of articles, lectures, and books on mentoring, many by J. Robert Clinton.

Center for Coaching & Mentoring offers a variety of articles on mentoring theory and research at www.coachingandmentoring.com.

"Church-based Mentoring: A Program Manual for Mentoring Ministries" and "The Mentor Training Curriculum," plus other mentoring resources, are available from the Points of Light Foundation, 1400 I Street, NW, Suite 800, Washington, DC 20005. E-mail: www.PointsofLight.org/volunteermarketplace

Clinton, J. Robert, and Richard W. Clinton. *The Mentor Handbook*. Altadena, CA: Barnabas Publishers, 1987. In-depth academic and systematic approach to mentoring, serving as an excellent expansion of concepts explained in *Connecting: The Mentoring Relations You Need to Succeed in Life*.

Joynet Mentoring Services, Joy Leadership Center, 21000 N. 75th Avenue, Building 16, Glendale, AZ 85308–9622. E-mail: www.joylead.org.

"Life to Life," workshop on mentoring by David Kraft, 2325 Joyce Drive, Palm Springs, CA 92261. E-mail: DKraft3851@aol.com.

Pastoral Leadership Institute, 550 N. Parkcenter Drive, Suite 204, Santa Ana, CA 92705-3528. E-mail: PLINCOesch@aol.com.

United States Coast Guard Mentoring Program Web site has a number of excellent articles on mentoring: www.uscg.mil/hq/g-w/g-wt/g-wt/mentoring.htm.

ATE DUE